Introduction

Porthmadog is a splendid seaside re Snowdonia National Park. Inland, ... town transformed from one of the world's greatest slate mining centres into a historic resort for visitors. Linking the two is the fascinating and lively **Ffestiniog Railway**, one of Wales' successful 'Great Little Trains', which passes through absolutely stunning scenery. It is a truly fascinating area for walkers, who can enjoy sweeping views, lakes and mountains, rivers and waterfalls, together with the stimulating, and in many cases 'living', remains of the industrial revolution.

Any of these walks can be undertaken by a reasonably fit person, with **Walks 9 & 10** being the most challenging. Walking boots or strong shoes are recommended for all of them, and *please* keep in mind that this is sheep farming country – *dogs must be kept on a lead at all times (or left behind)*.

The location of each route is shown on the back cover, and a full summary of the major characteristics and length of each is described on a special chart. An estimated time is also given, but for those who enjoy fine views and like to linger over them, or to further explore the fascinating industrial heritage, it is best to allow longer. This splendid environment is far too good to hurry through.

Each walk has a map and description which enables the route to be followed without further help, but always take account of the weather and dress accordingly, especially if you are exploring one of the higher routes. A weather forecast for the area can be obtained by calling 0891 505315 (charge).

Please respect local traditions, and always take special care of the environment, so that all those who wish to share the great charm and beauty of this magical part of Wales may continue to do so.

About the author, David Perrott . . .

Having moved with his wife Morag to Machynlleth from London some twenty years ago, his love of Wales remains as strong now as it was then. A member of the Machynlleth Ramblers' group, he still enjoys walking and cycling in Wales, a part of the British Isles which he believes manages to combine examples of splendid scenery and friendly people within an amazingly compact area.

WALK 1
THE LLOYD GEORGE MUSEUM

DESCRIPTION A mainly level 5½ mile walk which starts at Criccieth Castle and strikes out along the coast, then heads inland along the Afon Dwyfor to reach The Lloyd George Museum at Llanystumdwy. The return is along a very quiet minor road with fine views over Cardigan Bay. It would make a beautiful evening walk. Allow 3 hours.

START The lay-by by Criccieth Castle. SH 499378.

DIRECTIONS From the Tourist Information Centre in Porthmadog head west along the A497 for a little over 5 miles to Criccieth. Turn left in the town and drive over the railway to park by the castle. There is a British Rail service. Buses 1 & 3.

1 Leave the castle and walk with the sea to your left. When the road veers inland, go through a gate to join a path by the sea, and continue. When the road veers inland at Cefn Castell, turn LEFT to rejoin the path by the sea. The path descends to the beach at Ynysgain *where 200 acres of foreshore and a farm are owned by the National Trust*, then go through and walk with the river to your left. You soon rejoin the river: continue, going through a gate (with a signpost).

2 Cross a stile beside a gate, then head towards the next gate BUT DO NOT GO THROUGH. Continue with the fence on your right. At a break in the broken stone wall on your left,

3 You reach a gate and ladder stile. Cross it, turn RIGHT and walk with a fence on your right. Go through a gate, cross the stile by the next gate and CAREFULLY cross the railway. Cross the next stile and continue along the track. Cross a fence stile, then the step-stile close-by at *Aberkin*, and continue. Go through a gate and CAREFULLY cross the main road.

4 Go through a gate and continue along to the bridge at Llanystumdwy (*the church at the bend of the river*). Ignore the road to the right and continue ahead, with the river on your left. The entrance to the David Lloyd George Museum is on the right, opposite his grave. The pretty, and remarkably tidy, village of Llanystumdwy, standing astride

head inland beside the Afon Dwyfor (*Great Water*).

WALK 1

the Afon Dwyfor, was the childhood home of David Lloyd George, later Earl Lloyd George of Dwyfor (1863-1945). His early home still stands, next to a centre illustrating his life and times. Early years were spent practising as a solicitor in Manchester. Originally apprenticed to a non-trial lawyer in 1878, he started his own practice in 1884. Working as a poacher's lawyer he gained a loyal following defending those who had broken the punitive poaching laws of the time. He was elected Member of Parliament for Caernarfon in 1890, a seat he was to hold until a year before his death. Influenced by Welsh nationalism and industrial ownership during the 19thC, he introduced, as Chancellor in the Asquith Liberal administration 1908-11, social reforms which laid the earliest foundations for the welfare state. Opposition to his radical ideas from the House of Lords precipitated the general Election of 1911, and resulted in the influence of the Lords being curtailed, leaving the House of Commons as the sole authority. Although reluctant to condone Britain's involvement in the First World War, he became Munitions Minister 1915-16, and ensured a steady supply of weapons to the western front. Appointed Minister of War, he became Prime Minister during the latter part of the Great War. Victorious in the general election which followed, he seemed to find peace more difficult to manage than war. A treaty was conceded with the new Irish Free State in 1921 when attempts to suppress the revolution failed, but it seemed that this, amongst other difficulties, led to his defeat in the election of 1922. United with the Asquithian Liberals, he later succeeded Asquith, but with the decline of Liberalism he never held office again. A distinguished orator and author, he retained his use of the Welsh language throughout his life. Given an earldom, he died soon after on 26th March 1945. The centre is open 10.30-17.00 Easter, Apr-May Mon-Fri, June Mon-Sat, July-Sept daily, Oct 11.00-16.00 Mon-Fri. Closed Nov-Mar. Charge. Continue along the quiet lane until you reach 30mph signs, where you turn RIGHT. Continue to the main road, CAREFULLY cross it and continue to Marine Terrace (signposted). Turn LEFT at the seafront to return to the castle.

*C*riccieth Castle enjoys a magnificent situation, atop a rocky headland overlooking Cardigan Bay. It is a Welsh castle, first mentioned in 1239. The twin-towered guardhouse was built by Llywelyn the Great on the site of much earlier fortifications, and was used by him as a temporary prison for his son Gruffudd. The outer defences were built by Llywelyn the Last and, following his death in battle in 1282, the castle was taken by the English kings Edward I and II, and further improved in 1292 at a cost of over £500, with one of the towers being modified to accept a stone-throwing catapult. Besieged by the Welsh 1294-5, its position on the coast allowed it to be supplied by sea, and it survived. The story was different in 1404 however, when the castle was again besieged, this time by Owain Glyndwr. His allies, the French, cut of access by sea, and the castle fell. The walls still bear evidence of its burning at that time. It has never since been reoccupied. The name Criccieth may be derived from Crug Aeth – a sharp hill-top. The vague remains of a far more ancient fortification stand on Moel Ednyfed, to the north of the town. The castle is open 10.00-18.00 daily, and is in the care of CADW. Charge.

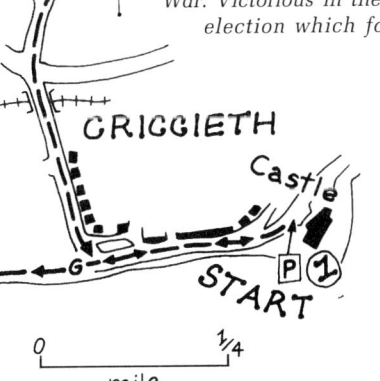

3

WALK 2
ABOVE PENMORFA

DESCRIPTION A steady climb on the initial part of this 3-mile walk is rewarded with an exploration of an ancient valley and superb views over Porthmadog. The return is along a good path down a wooded hillside. A nearby craftshop, farm museum and café is worth visiting. Allow 2½ hours.
START Lay-by at Penmorfa. SH 546406.
DIRECTIONS From Porthmadog, take the A487 to Tremadog, and turn left. After about 2 miles you reach Penmorfa. The lay-by is at the far end of the village, on the right, just beyond a chapel. Buses 1 & 2.

1 From the lay-by, walk towards the village, then take the first LEFT up Hen Lon. Follow the lane as it bends to the left, ignoring a footpath sign indicating to the right. After about ¼ mile, look out for a small metal gate up the bank on the RIGHT. Go through the gate and cross the field. Go through a gate and turn LEFT, to walk with a hedge on the left. The route bends to the right. Go through the next gate and cross a track to a stile. Cross the stile and continue ahead, with an old stone bank to the right.

2 Go through a small metal gate and follow the path uphill along the side of the garden of *Tyddyn Deucwm Ucha* to a rough fence stile in the corner. Cross it and continue uphill, with the fence to your right. Go through a small metal gate and turn LEFT, to walk with a wall on your left. You then pass through two gates to reach *Gesail Gyfarch*.

3 Turn RIGHT up the lane in front of the house, then turn RIGHT again up the track opposite the rear of the house. Walk up the field, and go through the opening in a stone wall, then walk towards the gate in the far right-hand corner of the field. Go through, then bear left to cross a ruined stone wall and go through a gate. Continue along the valley.

4 As you walk along the valley, look over to the left, where a fence curves away around a small hill topped with stones. You will see a stile in this fence. Walk to the stile, cross it and continue ahead, across a patch of boggy ground. Go through a gap in an old stone wall and continue, with higher ground to the right. Eventually you pick up a path which bends to the right to *Garth Farm*.

5 Go through the gate to the right of the farm house and turn RIGHT, to walk with a fence to the right. Cross a ladder stile ahead, situated where a fence and stone wall meet. Continue, crossing the next ladder stile over the stone wall ahead, then walk half-RIGHT uphill to another stile. Cross it and turn LEFT, to walk with a fence to the left. *Stunning views over Porthmadog and the Llyn Peninsula open up ahead.* Continue until you are level with *Cwm Mawr*, where a fence joins from the left.

6 Turn RIGHT here and start to descend. The path initially follows a narrow track, passing a small tree. Maintain your descent, soon picking up a conspicuous path. A fence joins from the left. Cross a ladder stile and continue. Cross the next ladder stile and carry on along the path. Go through a rough gate and continue.

7 Go through a small footpath gate to the left of a larger gate, and continue downhill. Cross a track by a house and maintain your direction downhill. Go to the right and then left around a corrugated iron shed to rejoin the main road. Turn RIGHT to return to the start.

*T*yn Llan, a craftshop, farm museum and café, is down the road which forks left. This lane was apparently once the main route for pilgrims travelling to Bardsey Island, and drovers making the journey with their cattle, sheep and geese in the opposite direction. Travellers used to wait at Tyn Llan for low tide before crossing the marshes below. It is open 09.30-18.00 daily Easter-October, and it is closed on Sundays in the low season.

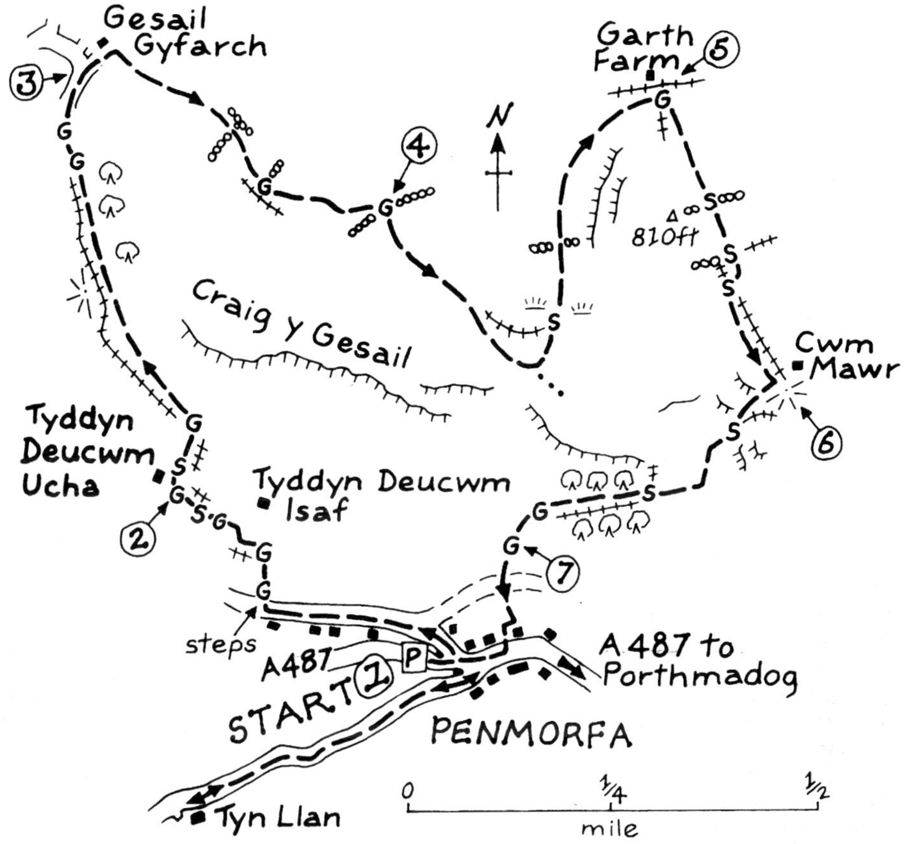

WALK 2

The church at Penmorfa contains a tablet dedicated to Sir John Owen, a 17thC Royalist leader. When condemned to death by the Parliamentarians, it is said that together with his fellow prisoners they drew lots to see who would survive this unfortunate fate. Sir John was lucky, and lived to see Charles II restored to the throne.

Tyn Llan

WALK 3
EXPLORING PORTHMADOG

DESCRIPTION This 2½ mile walk takes you up above Porthmadog for a splendid view over the estuary, before dropping down to Borth-y-Gest, passing the Maritime Museum and returning alongside the Afon Glaslyn to the pretty harbour. Allow about 2 hours.
START The Tourist Information Centre, Porthmadog. SH 570385.

1 From the Tourist Information Centre, walk to the LEFT along the main street. Turn LEFT at the roundabout along the A497, and, after a short distance, turn LEFT again up the footpath opposite the Snowdonia Press. Walk uphill through trees to reach a ladder stile, and cross it. The path climbs steeply through trees to join another path. Turn LEFT here and continue, ignoring a path which leaves to the right.

2 Cross a ladder stile and *enjoy the fine view ahead, looking out over the estuary.* Descend steeply to another ladder stile (take care – it has missing steps). Veer RIGHT and follow the path. Cross a stile beside a gate, then cross another stile ahead. descend a steep path and veer left to join the caravan park road.

3 Turn LEFT to walk on the park road, which bends to the right and soon leaves the caravan park and descends to the main road.

4 Turn RIGHT, cross the main road, and veer left into a minor road. Turn LEFT at a footpath sign. Go through a gate and continue to the next gate. Go through this gate and walk with a fence to your left. Go through the next gate to reach the seafront at Borth-y-Gest. *Borth-y-Gest is a quiet seaside village around a shallow bay. Some suggest it was from here, in the 12thC, that Madoc, son of Owain of Gwynedd, left to 'discover' America, long before Columbus' voyage.*

5 Turn LEFT, cross the road and walk up a path with steps, to the right of the road. Continue walking ahead to reach the road beside the Afon Glaslyn. Continue along the road, *looking out for Cei Ballast, an island built from the ballast dumped from incoming vessels before they took-on cargo.* Eventually you reach the square at Corn Hill. Veer RIGHT across the square and continue to the main road, *passing Porthmadog Maritime Museum, which is situated on Cei Oakley, in the last remaining slate shed on Porthmadog Harbour. The museum depicts the achievements of the local shipbuilders in constructing schooners known as 'Western Ocean Yachts', which were 'quite outstanding vessels, the ultimate development of the small wooden merchant ship in Britain', and their associated history. It is open at Easter, and daily from May Bank Holiday until the end of September (or by arrangement, telephone 01766 513736 or 512864). Modest charge.* Turn LEFT at the main road to return to the start.

Porthmadog *is a 'new' town, elegantly constructed in the 1820s around the equally new harbour, built to ship slate from the mines around Blaenau. Both came about as a result of The Cob, a grand embankment carrying the Ffestiniog Railway and which reclaimed some 70,000 acres of land from the vagaries of the tide. The whole scheme – town, harbour, embankment & railway – came to fruition as a result of the tireless efforts of William Alexander Madocks MP. Indeed the embankment, almost a mile long, cost around £100,000 to build, a vast amount of money at that time, raised with the assistance of Percy Bysshe Shelley and his wife Harriet, who stayed on Madocks estate at Tan-yr-Allt. Madocks, not content with these great achievements, followed them up in 1810 with the construction of Tremadog (which you may pass through on your way to Walk 2), a handsome town with fine buildings upon a wide main street. T. E. Lawrence, Lawrence of Arabia, was born at 'Woodlands', in Tremadog, in 1888.*
Porthmadog is now a lively tourist centre in an enviable setting at the northern end of Cardigan Bay.

WALK 3

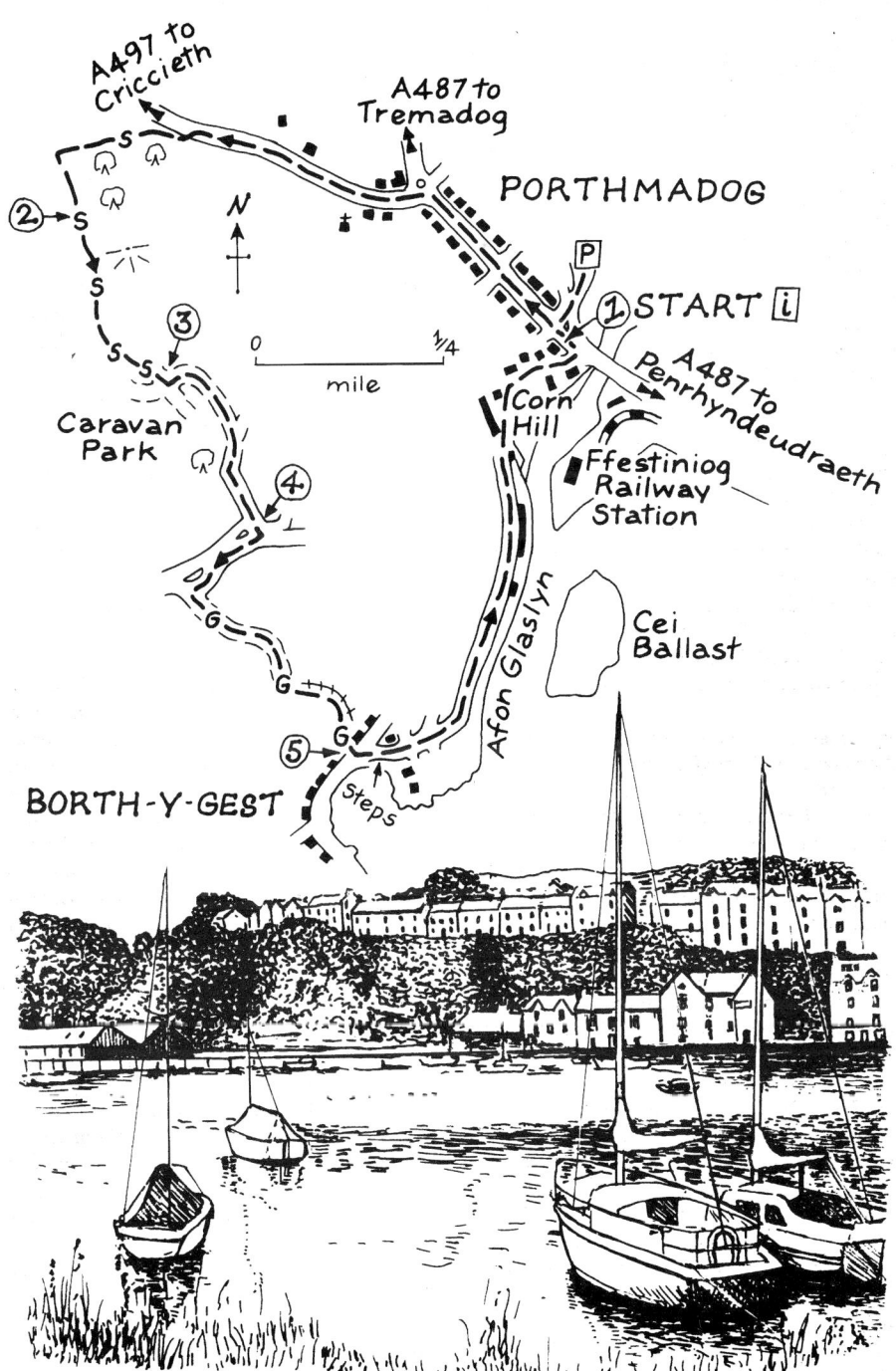

Porthmadog harbour

WALK 4
TY MAWR SLATE MILL

DESCRIPTION A fairly easy 2½-mile walk which follows the line of an old railway to the splendid remains of Ty Mawr Slate Mill, perhaps the most handsome in north Wales, before returning along the base of a dramatic rocky hillside and accross the dam of Cwmystradllyn. *Cwmystradllyn is a public water supply. Please respect it as such, and cause no pollution.* It is necessary to push through two or three overgrown conifers planted on the old railway line to keep to the recommended route to Ty Mawr, or alternatively you can by-pass this section by following a lane. Allow about 2 hours.

START From the parking area by the dam at Cwmystradllyn. SH 557442.

DIRECTIONS From the Tourist Information Centre in Porthmadog, take the A487 north to Tremadog and turn left. After about 3 miles turn right as signposted to Golan and Cwmystradllyn. A little under a mile further on, turn right as signed to Cwmystradllyn. Ignore a road which leaves to the right and continue until you reach the car park by the reservoir, passing the Slate Mill on the way.

1 From the parking area, walk back along the lane and turn LEFT at Tyddyn Mawr. Continue along the lane until you reach a ladder stile by trees on your left.

2 Turn LEFT, cross the stile and continue, pushing through the first two or three overgrown conifers. *If you find the trees intimidating, stay on the lane, which is quite pleasant, to reach the slate mill and rejoin the route there.* Cross two ladder stiles and carry on to cross a footbridge, go through a gate and continue to cross a step stile over a stone wall.

3 When you reach a gate, do not immediately go through, but turn RIGHT to visit *Ty Mawr Slate Mill*. Return to the path, go through the gate and turn LEFT. Follow the lane past the disused farm at *Ereiniog* and continue along the track, going through a gateway at *Ynys-wen*. Continue, forking LEFT, then immediately turning sharp LEFT. Walk beside a ditch towards the right hand side of some conifers.

4 Go through a small metal gate and continue ahead, leaving the trees over on your left. *It can be wet underfoot here.* Veer right to walk around the base of a hill. Approach a ladder stile avoiding another boggy patch, cross the stile and turn RIGHT. Go through a gate to rejoin the end of the dam, and turn LEFT to return to the start.

***T**y Mawr Slate Mill is a really splendid building, constructed between 1855-57 by Robert Gill and John Harris as part of the Gorseddau Quarry complex. It is an unusual three-storey design – most similar mills were long and narrow, with the slate moving horizontally through the various manufacturing processes. Power was provided by a 26 ft pitch-back water wheel, and the raw material was brought in by rail, and sawn and dressed within this exceptionally handsome building. Cisterns, tanks, wine coolers, grave-stones and clock faces were among the items made here, but the lack of waste heaps suggests it was not fully utilised, and it closed in 1877. It was later thought to have been used as a chapel, and an Eisteddfod was held here in 1888. It has been roofless since 1906.*

***C**wmystradllyn was a quite small, rather insignificant lake until 1960, when the dam was built, raising the level and creating the rather fine expanse of water we can see today. If you look beyond the dam, the man-made lake certainly looks quite natural, emphasising the basin which lies between Moel Hebog and Moel-ddu. On the slopes of Moel Hebog, that is directly to the north of the lake, are the barely discernable remains of hut circles: this was a very ancient human settlement.*

WALK 4

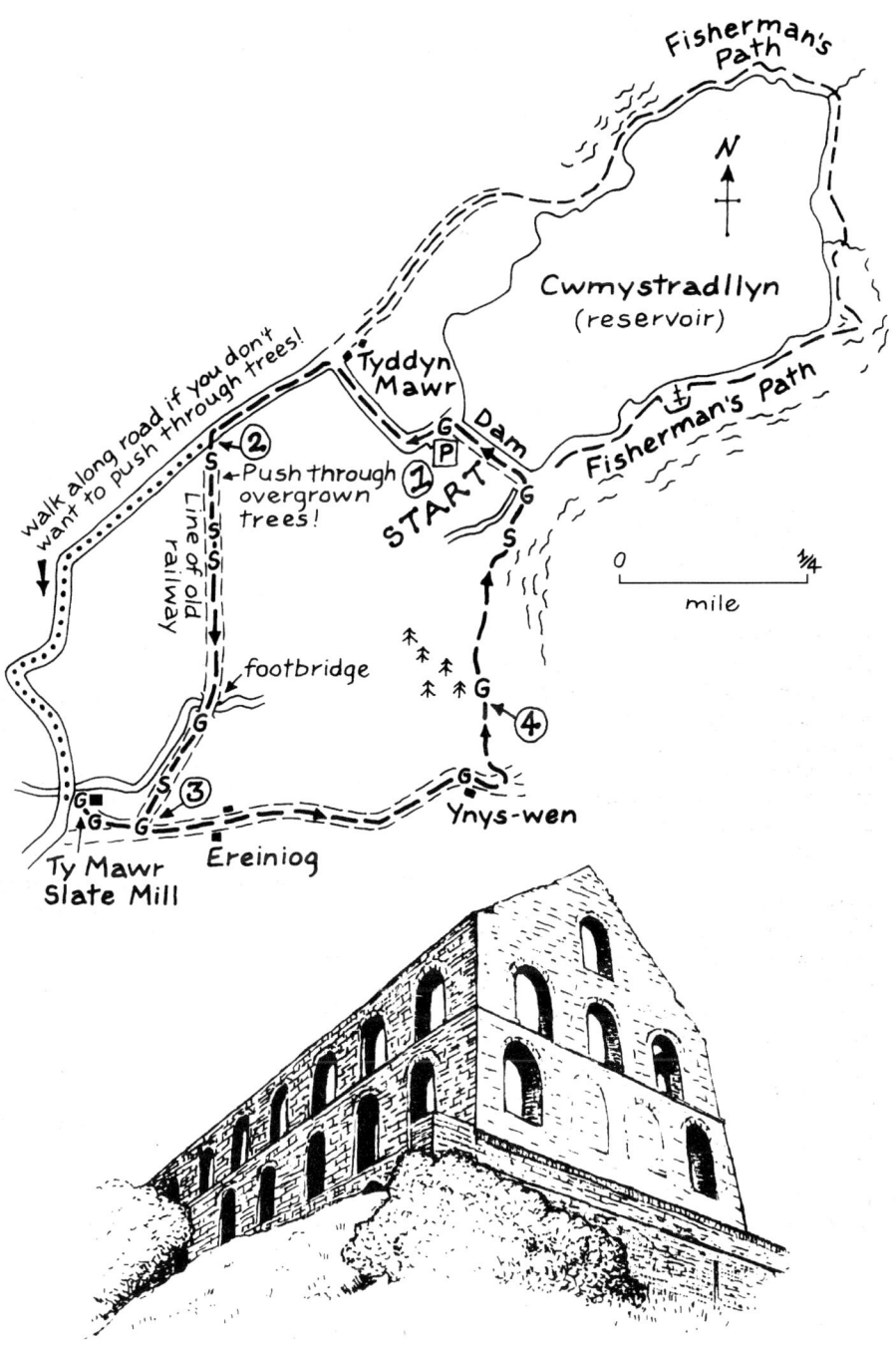

Ty Mawr Slate Mill

WALK 5
THE MAGIC OF PORTMEIRION

DESCRIPTION An easy 2½-mile walk which explores the countryside behind the magical village of Portmeirion. The route also visits Boston Lodge Halt on the Ffestiniog Railway, so there is always the chance of enjoying the sight of a passing steam train. Allow about 2 hours.

START The car park at Portmeirion. SH 589373.

DIRECTIONS From the Tourist Information Centre in Porthmadog, head east across The Cob on the A487. After 2 miles turn right as directed to Portmeirion, and park there. The walk can also start from Boston Lodge Halt, on the Ffestiniog Railway – also if you arrive on buses 1 or 2.

1 From the Portmeirion car park, walk away from the village to find the 'Footpath to Main Road' sign. Follow the path indicated. This eventually crosses a road and then turns RIGHT to follow the road. You soon reach footpath and bridleway signs indicating a road to the RIGHT. Follow this towards the estuary, then turn LEFT at a T junction.

2 When you reach a road, turn LEFT to walk to the main road. Cross this and walk down the minor road opposite, crossing the Ffestiniog Railway to reach a T junction. Turn LEFT and follow this quiet minor road until it joins the main road. Walk to the RIGHT along the main road and CAREFULLY cross it to reach Boston Lodge Halt.

3 Walk up the bridleway by Boston Lodge Halt. Walk beside the line, cross it carefully at the pedestrian level crossing and go over a stile beside a gate. The path then curves to the right and forks. Take the LEFT-hand fork. Climb up the track, go through a gate and continue to the next gate.

4 Go through the gate, cross a farm road and continue along the rough track ahead. Over to your right is Penrhyn-isaf where, on 7 September 1812 Thomas Edwards, a 65-year-old construction worker on the nearby Cob, murdered an 18-year-old maid Mary Jones. He stole £35 and a watch, and was hanged at Dolgellau on 7 April 1813. Go through an opening in a tall stone wall and continue, going through the next similar opening. Go through the gate ahead and continue along the track. You reach a ladder stile: DO NOT CROSS THIS. Turn RIGHT and continue, crossing a stile to return to the car park. The entrance to Portmeirion in over to the right.

It may seem odd to recommend coming to this corner of Wales to visit the re-creation of an Italian dream town, but Clough Williams-Ellis' extravaganza of Portmeirion, by the waters' edge, is far too good, and far too well done, to miss. Devoting his professional life to opposing the despoilation of the landscape, he purchased this site in 1928 and began its transformation, converting a 19thC house by the river into an elegant hotel, and topping a hill with a tall campanile (bell tower). In between there are domed villas, beautiful gardens, arches and walkways, and a town hall which contains a 17thC plastered ceiling rescued from a demolished Flintshire mansion. It could all so easily have been a tasteless indulgence, yet somehow the idea has been executed with such unselfconscious joy it has become one of North Wales' premier show-places. The whole is surrounded by fine wild gardens containing rare Himalayan flowering trees, situated on a spectacular stretch of coast. Naturally such an extravaganza has not gone unnoticed by the film and television industries. Amongst many dramas filmed here 'The Prisoner' is perhaps the most notable, commemorated by a small shop within the village, selling mementos of the series. Noel Coward wrote 'Blithe Spirit' in Portmeirion, in one week, staying in the Watch House. The hotel is expensive, but day visitors may enjoy the village between 09.30-17.30 daily for a modest charge.

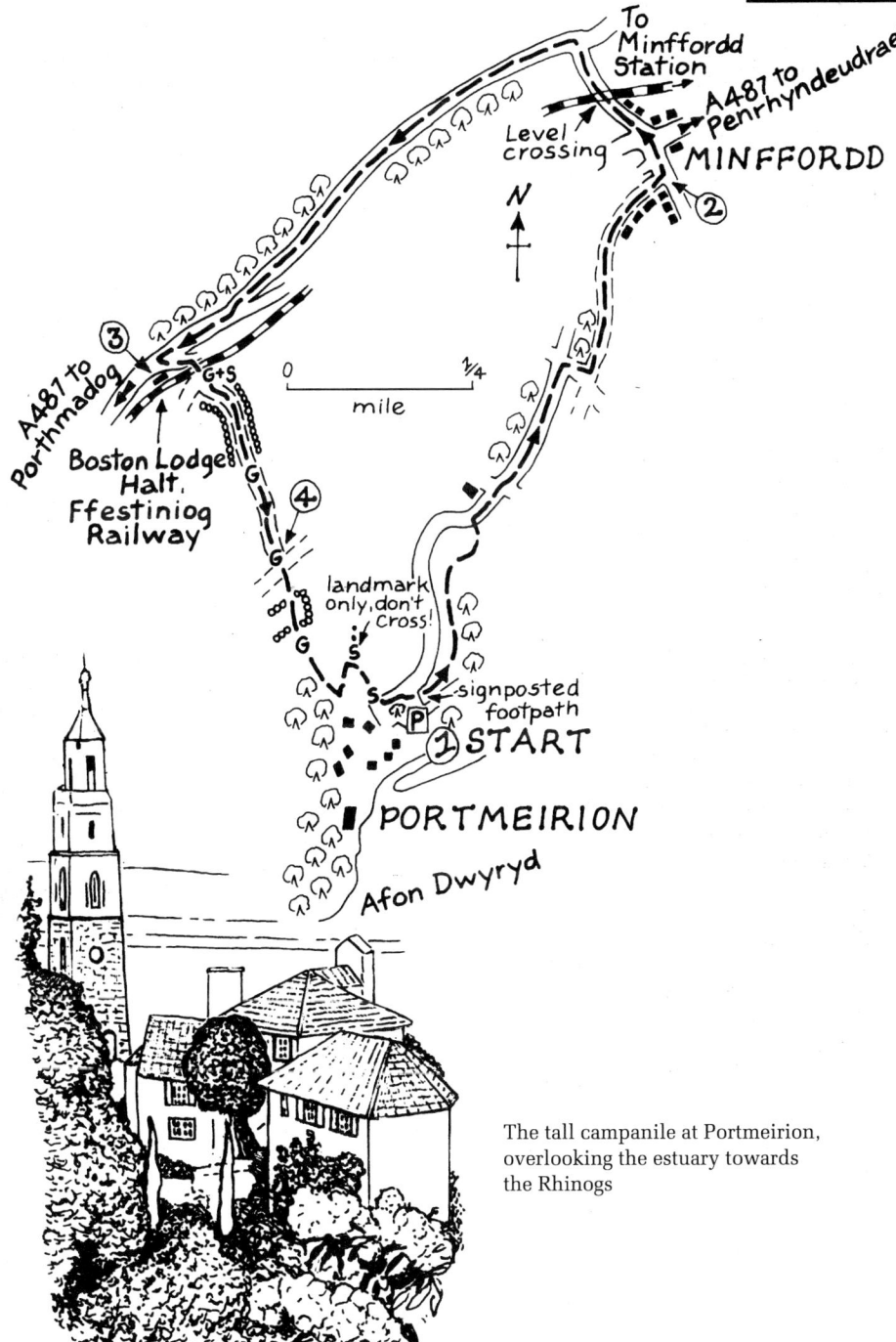

The tall campanile at Portmeirion, overlooking the estuary towards the Rhinogs

WALK 6
A RAMBLE FROM PENRHYN

DESCRIPTION A charming 2½ mile ramble in the peaceful countryside above Penrhyndeudraeth. The Ffestiniog Railway crosses the route twice. Allow about 2 hours.

START Near Penrhyn Station, above Penrhyndeudraeth. SH 614397.

DIRECTIONS From the Tourist Information Centre in Porthmadog, head east across The Cob on the A487. After 3 miles, turn left in Penrhyndeudraeth, and drive up the hill for a short way, to park in a cul-de-sac on the left, just beyond the level crossing, by the 30 mph signs. There is also a lay-by just a little further on. Or you can travel on the Ffestiniog Railway to Penrhyn Station.

1 From the cul-de-sac, turn LEFT onto a signposted path between stone walls. Go through a small gate, then turn LEFT to go through a second gate. Cross a muddy patch and bear left down to a wall. Walk with the wall on your right, turning RIGHT to follow the wall to a small metal gate. Go through the gate and turn LEFT, to go through another gate marked *Cae Merched*.

2 Immediately after going through the gate, veer half-RIGHT up a path (DO NOT follow the track). Cross the stone stile at the top and continue along the path in the direction indicated, winding through the gorse. Eventually you reach a ladder stile by a gate. DO NOT CROSS THIS, but follow the path to the RIGHT. The path bends right and left to reach a ladder stile. Cross this and continue with a wall to your left. The path descends steeply to go through a gap in an old stone wall. You reach a track.

3 Turn LEFT, go through a gate and then continue along the track. Eventually the track bends to the left. Continue ahead when a track leaves to the right over a cattle grid. You are now on a very minor road.

4 Turn LEFT off the road just below *Ty-obry*, and then turn LEFT again up a track. Go through the gate into woods and continue ahead for about 10 yards, then turn RIGHT as waymarked. Cross a stile by a gate, and continue through two small waymarked gates to join a lane. Continue along the lane.

5 When you reach the railway, turn LEFT downhill to go through a gateway. Turn RIGHT to go under the railway. After a short way turn LEFT up steps to follow the signposted footpath. Cross a stone step-stile and continue, ignoring a crossing over the railway. You emerge from the path beside a chapel. Continue ahead over a crossroads to reach the main road. Turn LEFT to pass Penrhyn Station and return to the start.

***P**enrhyndeudraeth* means 'the head of the hill-slope over the two reaches of sand': a glance at a map will show it is wedged between the estuaries of the Afon Glaslyn and Afon Dwyryd. The station on the Ffestiniog Railway is called Penrhyn, to distinguish it from the stop on the main Cambrian Coast line. Penrhyn Station was opened in 1865, and replaced with a larger building in 1879. When the railway was re-opened in 1957 this was, for a time, the line's terminus.

WALK 6

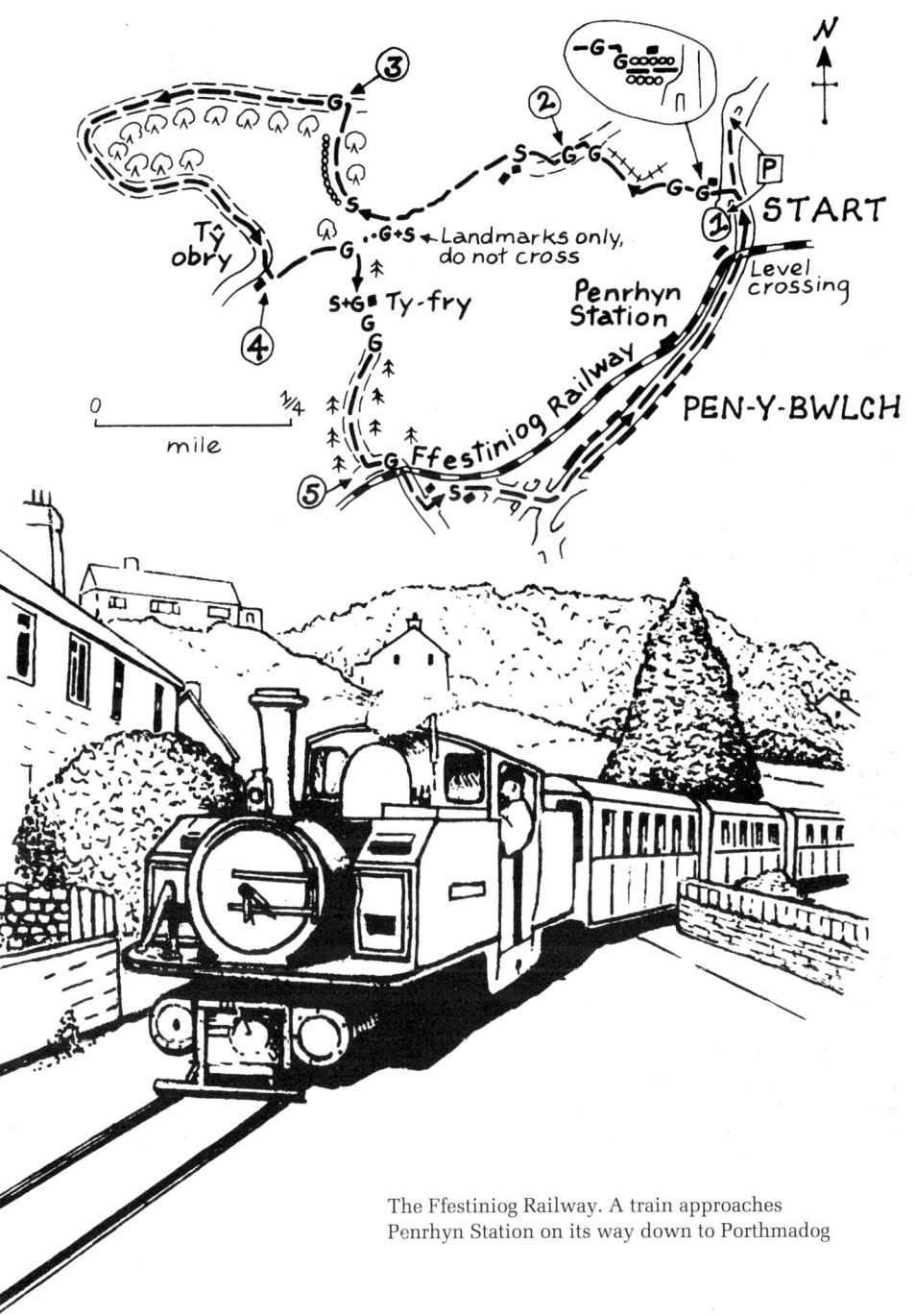

The Ffestiniog Railway. A train approaches Penrhyn Station on its way down to Porthmadog

WALK 7
LLANFROTHEN

DESCRIPTION An undulating 2½-mile walk from the ancient church at Llanfrothen through intimate woodlands and leading to expansive views over the Vale of Ffestiniog. Allow about 2 hours.

START From the roadside at Llanfrothen. SH 624413.

DIRECTIONS From the Tourist Information Centre in Porthmadog, take the A487 across The Cob. In Penrhyndeudraeth turn left onto the A4085. After a further 2 miles turn sharp right at Garreg onto the B4410. After half-a-mile turn sharp right to Llanfrothen. Pass through a gate across the road, and park carefully and considerately, causing no obstruction, by an old barn on the right.

1 From the barn, walk to the LEFT along the lane, passing back through the gate. Turn LEFT to walk between houses as signposted to the church. Walk around the churchyard wall, go through a small metal gate and pass a bijou residence to a second metal gate. Go through, turn RIGHT and follow the path ahead. Cross a small bridge over a stream and continue with a fence on the left (ignoring a gateway on the left). Walk up to a small metal gate and walk over well mown grass with a hedge on the left. Veer LEFT down a path to join a lane, which soon turns left to lead to a road.

2 Turn RIGHT and walk along the lane. When the lane bends slightly to the right, by an old concrete shed, turn LEFT up a waymarked path into trees. The path soon bends right and climbs, then goes left between trees. You emerge by a ruin. Walk around to the right of it then go LEFT through a waymarked gap in a wall. Continue climbing up the forestry road. When the track splits, go RIGHT and then immediately LEFT through trees to a ladder stile. Cross it and walk to the right down a small gully to a track.

3 Turn LEFT and walk ahead, ignoring a path off to the right. As you approach a ladder stile *look back for a splendid view over the estuary. The Ffestiniog Railway runs just below here so, if you are lucky, you may also see a steam train.* Cross the ladder stile and continue ahead, soon forking left as waymarked. Carry on ahead to reach a ruined building on the left.

4 Turn LEFT as waymarked just beyond the ruin, and follow the narrow path through trees and up a slope. Go through a gap in a stone wall and continue to the left through trees to a ladder stile. *There is yet another splendid view from here.* Turn RIGHT and walk downhill, keeping the slate waste tips to your right. When you reach the wall at the bottom of the field, walk to the right.

5 When you reach an improvised metal gate, turn LEFT and go through, then bear RIGHT, soon passing between a house and a rusty barn. Follow the track ahead, ignoring a waymark to the right. Go through the gate and turn LEFT on a path. Step over a ditch and continue downhill. Cross a stile and continue. Cross the stile on your LEFT and walk down the driveway, with a house to your left. Cross another stile to return to the start.

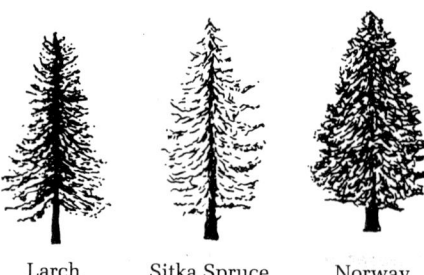

Larch   Sitka Spruce   Norway Spruce

St Brothen's Church *was the scene of a famous dispute in 1888. Robert Roberts, a non-conformist quarryman who died in that year, had asked to be buried here, as permitted under the Osborn Morgan Burial Act of 1881. The Rev. Richard Jones refused*

WALK 7

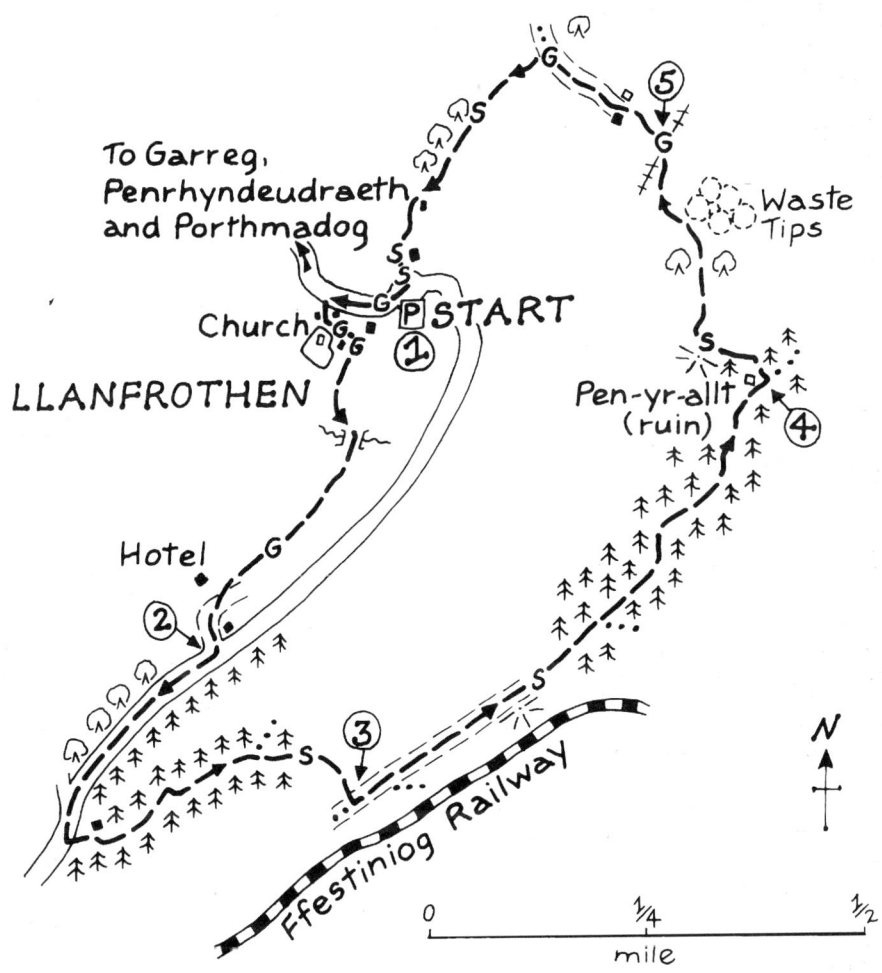

however, as the new part of the churchyard had been given in 1864 with the proviso that only Anglicans were to be buried there. As a result the churchyard gates were forced, the grave dug, and many people followed the coffin. Those responsible were summoned by the rector, but Lloyd George acted in their defence and they were acquitted. After a delay of two months, damages were awarded to the plaintiffs and costs to the defendants. Lloyd George appealed and the prosecution case was dismissed in London in December 1888. On the western side, now blocked, is an old Celtic door, designed to ensure that those entering were forced to stoop and bow. John Savin, the contractor of the Cambrian Railway, is buried nearby.

WALK 8
TANYGRISIAU RESERVOIR

DESCRIPTION An easy 3-mile walk which encircles Tanygrisiau Reservoir. The Ffestiniog Railway provides a colourful accompaniment on this route, and the Hydro Electric Power Station, and the feeder reservoir created by the Stwlan Dam high above, make an excellent and instructive visit. Allow about 3 hours.

START Car parks at the entrance to Tanygrisiau Power Station or Tanygrisiau Railway Station. SH 682450.

DIRECTIONS From the Tourist Information Centre in Porthmadog take the A487 across The Cob. After about 7 miles turn left onto the A496. After a further 3½ miles turn left, then left again, into Ffestiniog Power Station. Or you can arrive by steam train on the Ffestiniog Railway, and alight at Tanygrisiau.

1 Walk along the road with Tanygrisiau Reservoir to your left, passing the power station reception and café on your right. At a road junction, turn RIGHT, and then LEFT up the gated lane. Walk past the gate, CAREFULLY go over the level crossing and carry on ahead (*under NO circumstances should you walk along any part of the railway track*). When the lane bends to the right, take the track to the LEFT, signposted with a fish.

2 Cross the footbridge and ladder stile and continue downhill. CAREFULLY cross the railway line using the two ladder stiles and continue, walking to the RIGHT, beside the railway. Descend beside the power station fence, and follow the path to the left of a pylon, to walk with the lake on your left. After a short while a concrete road branches to the RIGHT. Follow this up to the railway and turn LEFT. Turn RIGHT to CAREFULLY cross the railway by two stiles (the second is broken). Turn LEFT and continue along the path, going gently uphill.

3 The path climbs through the remains of Moelwyn Mine, continuing uphill beside a stream and through a stone arch. Cross a wooden footbridge and follow the path to a gap in a stone wall on the left. Go through and continue along the path, gradually descending towards a large broken stone 'wall', which the railway passes through. *This broken stone structure was originally the dam of a reservoir, built in 1836, to provide water power for an incline on the original Ffestiniog tramway, at the time when waggons were pulled up to Blaenau Ffestiniog by horse, and came down by gravity. The New Moelwyn Tunnel beyond was built by the Ffestiniog Railway Society as part of the major deviation works caused by the construction of the reservoir and the power station. The first train ran through the tunnel on 7th February 1977.*

4 CAREFULLY cross two ladder stiles over the railway and continue, veering slightly left. Cross a track and carry on, walking gently uphill and then down, through heather. The path skirts a marshy inlet of the lake, then climbs a short rocky stretch up to a fence. Continue with the fence to your right and the lake over on your left.

5 The path veers away from the fence to join a track. Turn RIGHT to cross the brow of the hill. *This gives a fine view over the lake to the mountainside above the power station, where there are old workings, the Stwlan Dam which feeds the power station, and a quarry incline which passes through a tunnel into workings. The Ffestiniog Railway runs along the base of the mountains.* Just before you are directly opposite the power station the path splits – take the LEFT fork downhill, and follow the path around to the right.

6 You reach a conspicuous ladder-stile over a wall. Cross it and continue ahead, following the path through heather. The path joins a stony track for a short way, then branches off LEFT to descend the hillside, continuing roughly parallel to the outlet stream over on the left.

WALK 8

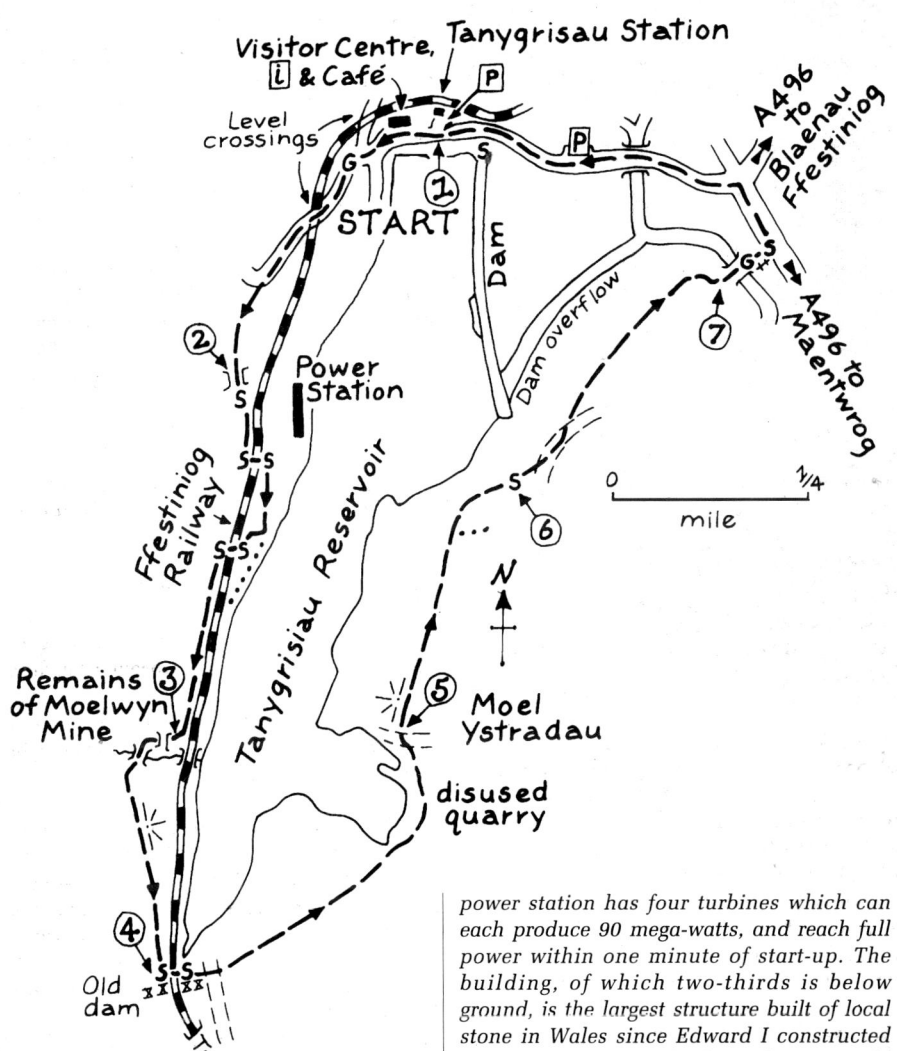

7 Veer left to a footbridge, cross it, go through a gate and continue ahead to a stile. Cross it and turn LEFT, then turn LEFT again to enter the access road to the power station and return to the start.

*F**festiniog Power Station* is available to generate hydro-electricity at times of peak demand, returning water to the upper reservoir, Stwlan, when demand is low. The power station has four turbines which can each produce 90 mega-watts, and reach full power within one minute of start-up. The building, of which two-thirds is below ground, is the largest structure built of local stone in Wales since Edward I constructed his castles at Harlech and Criccieth. Tanygrisiau Reservoir was created by building a dam 1800 ft long, with a height of almost 50 ft. The water level in the lake rises and falls about 18 ft during the power station's generating cycle. Stwlan, the upper reservoir, has a splendid dam some 800 ft long and 120 ft high. It is 1650 ft above sea level. You can visit the power station on an hourly guided tour. It is open daily in the high season, closed on Sundays May-Sept, and closed weekends in winter. There is a modest charge.

WALK 9
BLAENAU FFESTINIOG: ONE ON THE SLATE

DESCRIPTION An exciting 4-mile walk which visits slate mines high in the mountains above Blaenau Ffestiniog. An initial steep climb soon leaves the village behind and takes you through a fine mixture of industrial archaeology and stunning scenery, with extensive views beyond Trawsfynnydd. Allow about 3 hours.

START The station car park in Blaenau Ffestiniog. SH 700450.

DIRECTIONS From the Tourist Information Centre in Porthmadog, take the A487 across The Cob. After about 7 miles turn left onto the A496. Turn right at the roundabout in Blaenau Ffestiniog. The station car park is on the right. Or you can have an exciting ride up on the Ffestiniog Railway, or arrive on buses 1 or 3.

1 From the station car park in Blaenau Ffestiniog turn RIGHT onto the main street and walk along it. Just beyond the 'Job Centre', on the left-hand side of the road, turn LEFT and walk uphill, soon leaving the cottages behind, and passing between slate tips. The tarmac ends at metal gates. Go through the pedestrian gate and continue. *As the track climbs, look back for a superb view over Trawsfynnydd and beyond.* The track bends to the left and joins another. Continue ahead along the main track.

2 About 25 yards before a gate and cattle-grid cross the track, turn RIGHT up a stony track. Continue ahead when a track joins from the left. When the track forks, go LEFT. Go through two gates and continue along the track, to go through another gate. Continue ahead for about 50 yards.

3 Look for a waymark on a fence post over to your right, and turn RIGHT to walk in the direction indicated, keeping to the right of the hillside. Cross a stream, cross a stile by an electricity pole and continue uphill towards a conspicuous old pipeline. When you reach the pipeline, turn LEFT to walk steeply uphill, with the pipeline to your right. Walk to the right of the concrete building at the top and follow the slate slabs covering the leat (water-course). Go to the left of the pipe on a narrow path under a small crag. *You are now on open moorland above the quarries.* Follow the pipeline, which soon becomes a leat, with slate slabs covering it in places.

4 Join a track which comes in from the right from a ruined winding house, and continue ahead. *This track was once a railway – wooden sleepers are still embedded in its surface.* Continue along the track, going through a gate. *Look back for a superb view, and notice the leat still running beside the track. Where two leats join, the dam of Llyn Newydd is over to your left. You can walk over for a look at the reservoir but don't stop for too long, as the next expanse of water is much more attractive.* Return to the track and continue, crossing a very fine stone viaduct to the right of the dam. Continue, walking along the dam of Llyn Bowydd *an altogether more pleasing expanse of water, nestling amongst rocky outcrops.*

WALK 9

5 Immediately the dam ends, and before the track enters an attractive rocky cutting, turn RIGHT down a feint path at the base of a steep slope. Continue ahead over a low rocky summit. A wall comes in from the left. Continue beside the wall as the path descends to a double stile in the wall/fence now on your left. Turn LEFT, cross the stiles and turn RIGHT to walk with the wall/fence on your right for a short way, then veer LEFT towards the left-hand end of conspicuous stone tips (and avoiding a boggy patch of ground if necessary).

6 Cross a ladder stile and walk down to Llyn y Drum-boeth. Cross a stile and continue along the path to the right of a small pool and along the summit of a spoil heap. *The view from here presents a stunning vista of the country to the south-west.* Now carefully descend the end of the spoil heap and continue ahead, descending through heather towards a ruined winding-house.

7 CAREFULLY walk down the old incline to reach a stone shed on the right. Turn LEFT here to continue down slate steps and follow the clear path around to the right. The path descends through an old wall *with a fine view of Blaenau Ffestiniog ahead,* and crosses a SLIPPERY patch – TAKE CARE. As you approach a conifer plantation, veer to the RIGHT of it and follow the path down to a gate.

8 Go through the gate, walk down to a track and turn LEFT. Then, after about 15 yards, turn RIGHT through a small metal gate, with a spoil heap to the right. Go left when the path reaches a field corner and continue downhill, joining a road and heading towards a post box in a wall. Turn RIGHT at the main road to return to the start.

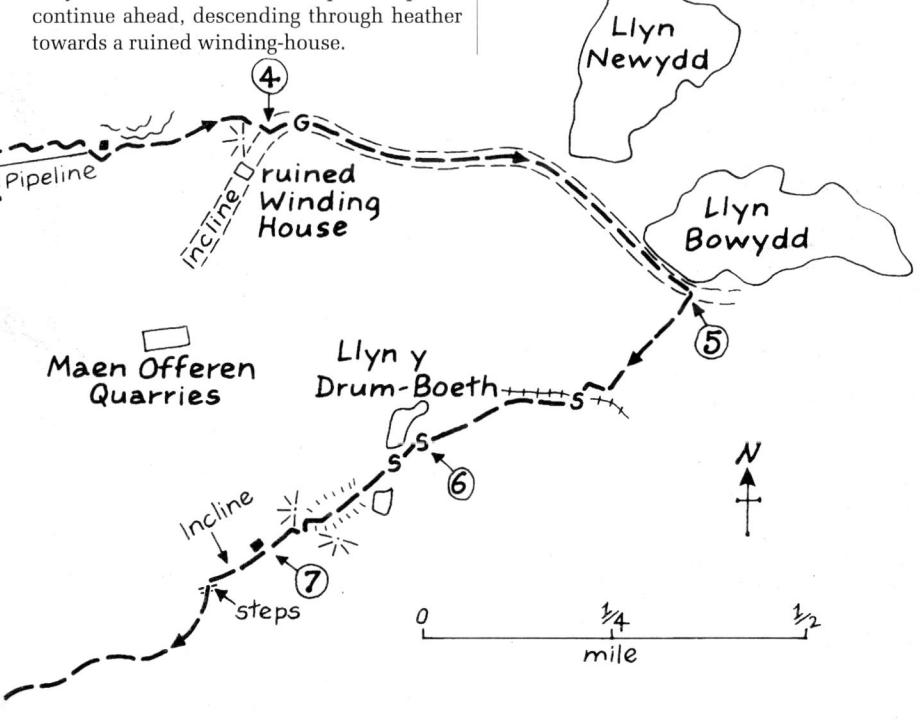

WALK 10
LLYN MORWYNION & RHAEADR-Y-CWM

DESCRIPTION This splendid 5½-mile walk starts at a height of over 1250 ft, above Rhaeadr-y-Cwm, and initially visits the wonderfully isolated Llyn Morwynion, a lake of legends. The path then descends 650 ft, giving absolutely splendid views to the west, before climbing beside the Afon Cynfal to the dramatic Rhaeadr-y-Cwm falls. *An initial short section of this walk can be wet underfoot.* The walk can also be shortened by starting from the viewpoint/layby on the B4391. Allow about 4 hours.

START The parking area on the B4407 by Llyn Dubach, about 2½ miles east of Ffestiniog. SH 746424.

DIRECTIONS From the Tourist Information Centre in Porthmadog take the A487 across The Cob. After about 7 miles turn left onto the A496. A little over a mile further on fork right onto the B4391. In Ffestiniog fork right onto the A470 then, immediately after the railway bridge, turn sharp left onto the B4391. Just over 2½ miles further on, turn left at Pont yr Afon-Gam, by the old petrol station, onto the B4407, and park by Llyn Dubach on the left.

1 Walk along the track to the left of Llyn Dubach towards a conspicuous white post. Cross a broken stile to the right of this post, and continue with a fence on your left. It can be boggy here. The fence bends to the left and soon you reach a stile. Cross it and walk down to *Llyn Morwynion, a lonely and beautiful expanse of water, The Lake of the Maidens. This refers to Blodeuedd and her Maidens of Arudwy, who supposedly drowned here when fleeing from Gwydion, although another version of the story has it that the women had become attracted to the Men of Arudwy after being carried off by them but, when the Men of Clwyd came to reclaim them, they threw themselves into the lake in despair.* Continue with the lake to your right. Cross a ladder stile and continue until the path reaches the end of the south side of the lake.

2 The path now veers away from the lake. Follow the path across a track and continue until you pass under a line of electricity poles. Now leave the conspicuous path and walk just to the left of the poles. Soon the track improves, and a wall joins on the left. Continue, now on a better track, to veer to the left down to a gate. Go through and turn RIGHT to walk along the road, until you reach gates facing each other across the road.

3 Turn LEFT, go through the gate and follow the track. When the track splits, go RIGHT through a gateway, then turn LEFT keeping parallel to an old wall. Go through a gap in a field corner and turn RIGHT, to walk with a fence on the right.

4 You reach a gate. Go through, and follow the track. Go through another gate, descend the track, climb another gate and carry on. Go through a farmyard and a gate and continue downhill. Go through a gate and turn LEFT onto a minor road.

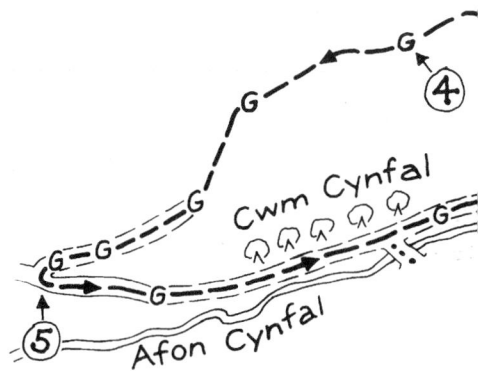

WALK 10

5 Walk along the minor road through Cwm Cynfal, passing through three gates to reach *Cwm Farm*, and ignoring any branches off. DO NOT go through the yard, but walk to the left of the fence to the ladder stile ahead. Cross it and turn LEFT. The path now climbs steeply and bears to the right, soon giving excellent views of *Rhaeadr-y-Cwm, the Waterfall of the Valley, which drops some 400 ft in six spectacular leaps down a narrow ravine.* Continue along the path, which runs parallel to the road, and is boggy in places. Ignore the first gate on the left, but go through the second smaller gate.

6 Join the road and turn RIGHT. Cross a cattle grid and continue to reach *Pont-yr-Afon Gam, which was reputedly Wales' highest filling station, at 1250 ft.* Turn LEFT along the B4407 to return to the start.

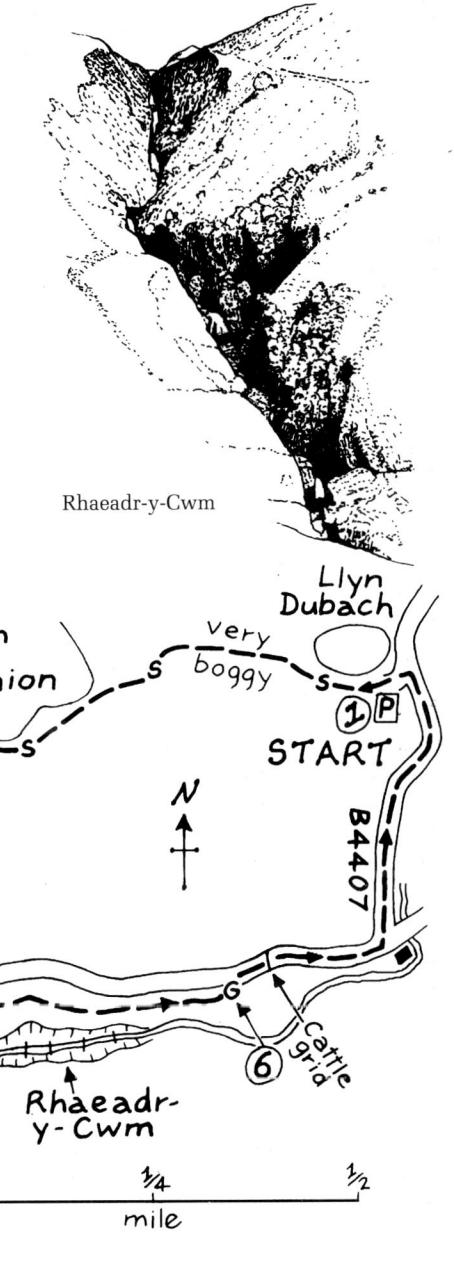

Rhaeadr-y-Cwm

WALK 11
RHAEADR CYNFAL:
THE CYNFAL WATERFALL

DESCRIPTION An easy 2½-mile walk which visits a splendid waterfall, then continues through a fine wooded and steep sided valley. The return crosses a small hill which affords splendid views towards Ffestiniog and the mountains to the north. Allow 2 hours.
START By the church in Ffestiniog. SH 701420.

DIRECTIONS From the Tourist Information Centre in Porthmadog, take the A487 across The Cob. After about 7 miles, just after the road crosses the Afon Dwyryd, turn left onto the A498. A little over a mile further on, fork right onto the B4391 to Ffestiniog. Park in the village below the church, in front of the Pengwern Arms Hotel. Or take bus 1.

1 Walk to the RIGHT along the main road, then soon turn LEFT through a metal gate signed to Rhaeadr Cynfal Falls. Continue ahead, then turn LEFT through a swing gate and walk half-RIGHT down to a metal gate.

2 Go through the metal gate, cross a little bridge and follow the path to another metal gate. Go through and walk with a wall on your left. Go through a wooden gate and turn RIGHT. Go through another metal gate and veer to the left to an opening in a fence/wall. Go through and turn LEFT. Continue, going through a gap in a wall and continuing gently downhill, with a wall on your left.

3 Reach a ladder stile and cross it. The path which forks immediately right leads to a viewpoint over the waterfalls. Here you will see a fine arch of water falling into a gloomy fissure, overhung with trees. Downstream is a column of rock known as Huw Llwyd's Pulpit. Huw Llwyd lived in Cynfal Fawr, to the south, and came here during the 17thC to preach, recite poetry and practise the raising of the devil. He felt safe to do this here as the devil could not apparently swim, and did not like to get his feet wet. Huw's activities were recorded by Thomas Love Peacock (1785-1866) in his novel Headlong Hall. This was also a resting place for about 120 workers at the Blaenau Ffestiniog quarries as they journied to and from their homes at Trawsfynydd on Saturday evening and Monday morning.

Their voices could be heard from far away, as if coming from 'a monster beehive'. Rhaeadr Cynfal is within the Ceunant Cynfal National Nature Reserve. Return to the path and turn RIGHT, to descend steps to a bridge, with a gate. Cross the bridge and climb steps up the far side.

4 Cross the stile on the RIGHT at the top of the steps and walk ahead, following the feint path, which veers away from the falls to a small metal gate. Go through and continue

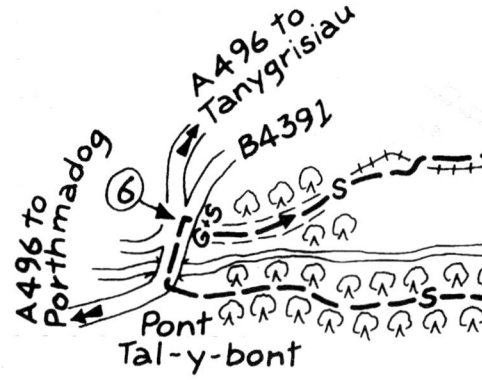

to a stile. Cross this and follow the path, with a fence over to your right. Cross a stile and walk down to a second stile. Cross this stile and follow the path downhill. The route winds amongst trees and goes through an elaborate wrought iron gate. Continue along the path, crossing a stile over a broken fence and eventually emerging at a road. Turn RIGHT and cross the bridge.

WALK 11

6 Turn RIGHT immediately after the bridge to cross a way-marked stile, and follow the track. Soon the track forks: take the LEFT fork up to a stile. Cross this and continue ahead, with a broken wall on the left. Go through a gap in the broken wall and continue with the wall now on your right, towards an electricity pylon. When the path forks, go to the RIGHT through a gap in the broken wall, and continue with the wall on your left, and the pylon to the right. *There is an excellent view of the mountains to the north. On the summit of the small hill to the right is an insignificant monument to William Charles IV, Baron Newborough, who died 19 July 1916, aged 42 years.* Go through a gate and continue through a second gate to reach the road. Turn RIGHT to return to the start. *There is a fine viewpoint, with seats, above the church in Ffestiniog. You can see the sea from it.*

Huw Llwyd, who is mentioned at point 3, actually made his living by being what we would understand today to be a wizard, or a conjuror. Such people were relatively common in North Wales during the 17thC, claiming to be the seventh son of a seventh son. Some wizards sold their souls to the devil by taking a mouthful of water from a holy well and immediately spitting it out, putting them in contact with the devil. Although well-educated, Huw found that being a wizard renumerated him richly in the midst of a largely illiterate population. There was, however, one farmer who did not take seriously Huw's incantations from his pulpit, and shouted abuse. Huw promptly cursed the man and, true to form, several days later, his cattle started to die. Totally distraught, the man begged Huw's forgiveness. This was given, for a fee of course, and soon everything returned to normal.

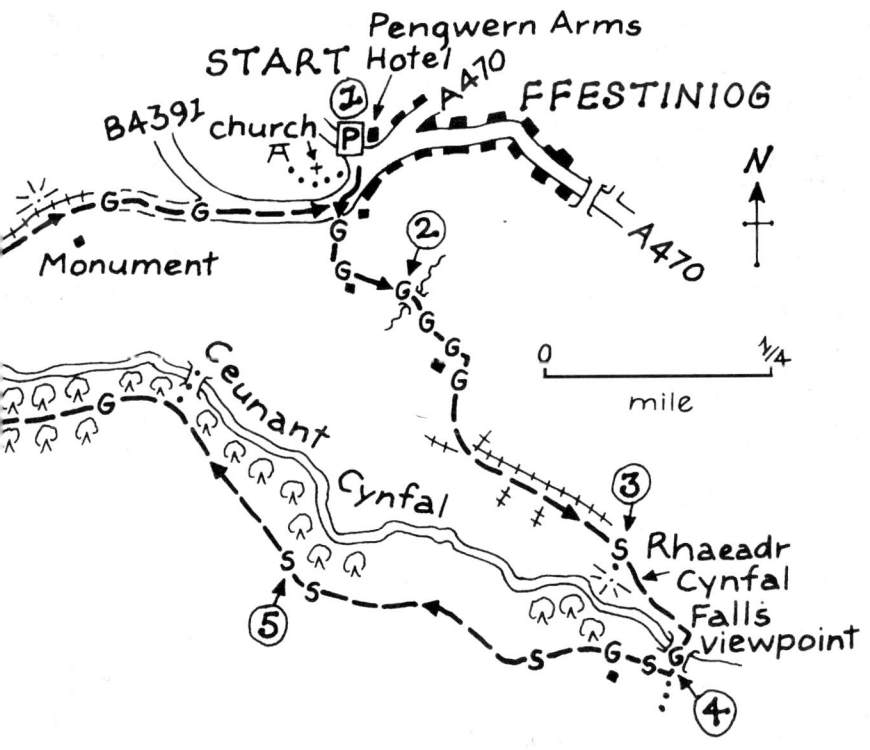

WALK 12
IN ROMAN FOOTSTEPS

DESCRIPTION A 4½-mile walk, which can easily be shortened to 3½ miles by taking an alternative starting point. The route encircles the prominent remains of a Roman fort and amphitheatre, visits a peaceful lake and affords splendid views over Llyn Trawsfynydd. Allow about 3 hours for the full walk.

START The lay-by opposite the entrance to Trawsfynydd Nuclear Power Station, SH 697385, or the lay by at SH 708389 for the shorter walk.

DIRECTIONS From the Tourist Information Centre in Porthmadog, take the A487 across The Cob. After 9½ miles park in the lay-by opposite the entrance to Trawsfynydd Nuclear Power Station, or take bus 2 or 3.

1 Take the signposted footpath at the north end of the lay-by, going down steps. Follow the path (shared with a stream!) under the railway, cross a stile and follow the generously way-marked path through trees. The route bends left and right, passing under power lines. stones (great fun for young children). Cross a stone bridge over a small stream. Cross another stile and a bridge and walk over a patch of gravel covered ground. Go through wide gates and turn RIGHT onto a lane, to reach a lay-by.

2 Cross a second stile and walk with the fence on your right. Go through a gate in the field corner and now walk with the fence on your left. The power lines are soon left behind as you cross a stile and carry on ahead, crossing a field following way-marked

24

WALK 12

3 *This is the starting point for the shorter walk.* Continue along the lane, passing the Roman Amphitheatre on the right. *This circular, embanked and grassy enclosure is all that remains of what is thought to be a Roman Amphitheatre, built in the 1st century AD. It is the only such construction attached to an auxiliary fort in Britain, although some doubt whether it was a true amphitheatre at all. It is indeed quite small and was probably used for weapons training.* Continue over a cattle grid and then, after about 50 yards, fork RIGHT along a signed track (ignore another track just before this one). Follow the track, passing to the right of Llyn yr Oerfel and to the left of the line of an old tramway. The track passes through the remains of *Braich-ddû quarries* and becomes grassy. *There are fine views over Llyn Trawsfynydd and the mountains beyond.* It finally descends to the pretty ruins of Dolbelydr farm, overlooked by a waterfall.

4 Turn RIGHT by *Dolbelydr* and follow the track *on the course of a Roman road.* Go through a gate and continue under power lines, curving to the right and joining a wall on the left.

5 The track bends to the LEFT and goes through a gate to reach *Llwyn-crwn* farm. Pass through 6 gateways to emerge on a farm road (courtesy path). Walk down the road to the old railway bridge.

6 DO NOT go under the bridge, but turn sharp RIGHT along a signposted, walled, track. Cross a little stream and go through a gate. Turn RIGHT to walk uphill towards power lines. Veer slightly left to go through a gate, and continue ahead. Ford a stream and veer left to a gate below a pylon.

7 Go through the gate and veer left to walk with a wall on your right. You descend to a gateway on your right. Go through, turn left, ford the stream (look for the easiest place) and follow the track, with a wall on your left. Go through the next gate and continue to another gate, and go through. *This level area was once a Roman parade ground.*

8 Turn sharp LEFT through a gate to reach a ruined farm, built on the line of the walls of a Roman Fort. Return along the track, go through the gate and turn LEFT to walk past the amphitheatre to the road. Turn LEFT to retrace your steps to either starting point.

This Roman fort was originally constructed in 78 AD after Agricola's campaign, then modified and reduced in size around 120 AD under Hadrian, and finally abandoned in 140 AD. The rebuilding was well recorded in a series of ten centurial stones, which signified the completion of a section of wall by 100 soldiers. These stones were recovered in the 19thC, and one of them is apparently built into the doorway of The Grapes Hotel at Maentwrog. The prominent mound of Tomen-y-Mur was built much later, and is all that remains of a Norman motte and bailey fortification. There is little knowledge of its origins, although it is known to have been associated with William Rufus in 1095. Access to the site is by agreement between the landowner and the National Park Authority, and depends upon responsible use by visitors.

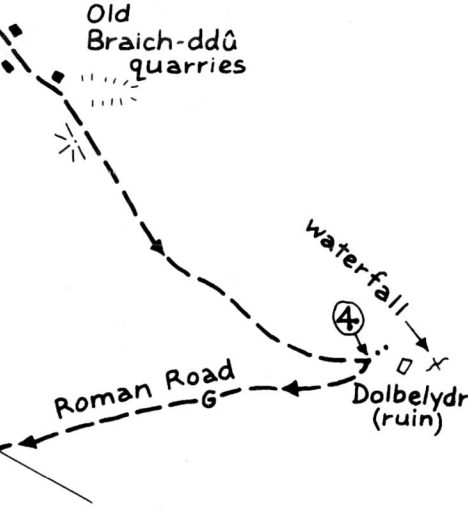

WALK 13
RHAEADR-DDU: THE BLACK WATERFALL

DESCRIPTION This gentle and wooded 3½-mile route visits the splendid Rhaeadr-ddu, hidden in the beautifully overgrown Ceunant Llyfnant, a National Nature Reserve. The return explores the peaceful hills to the south of the Vale of Ffestiniog. Allow 2½ hours.
START The car park in Gellilydan. SH 685397.
DIRECTIONS From the Tourist Information Centre in Porthmadog, take the A487 across The Cob. Stay on this road and, after about 7 miles, turn sharp right into Gellilydan. There is a car park on the left, in the village centre. You can take bus no. 2.

1 Rejoin the road and turn RIGHT. Turn RIGHT again by the *Pen-y-bont* stores and continue along this quiet lane, passing the *Bryn Arms* pub. When the lane turns to the right at *Bryntirion*, go to the left along the track and through a gateway.

2 The track soon splits. Go to the RIGHT and continue. Pass through a gate, ignoring a track off to the left. Go through another

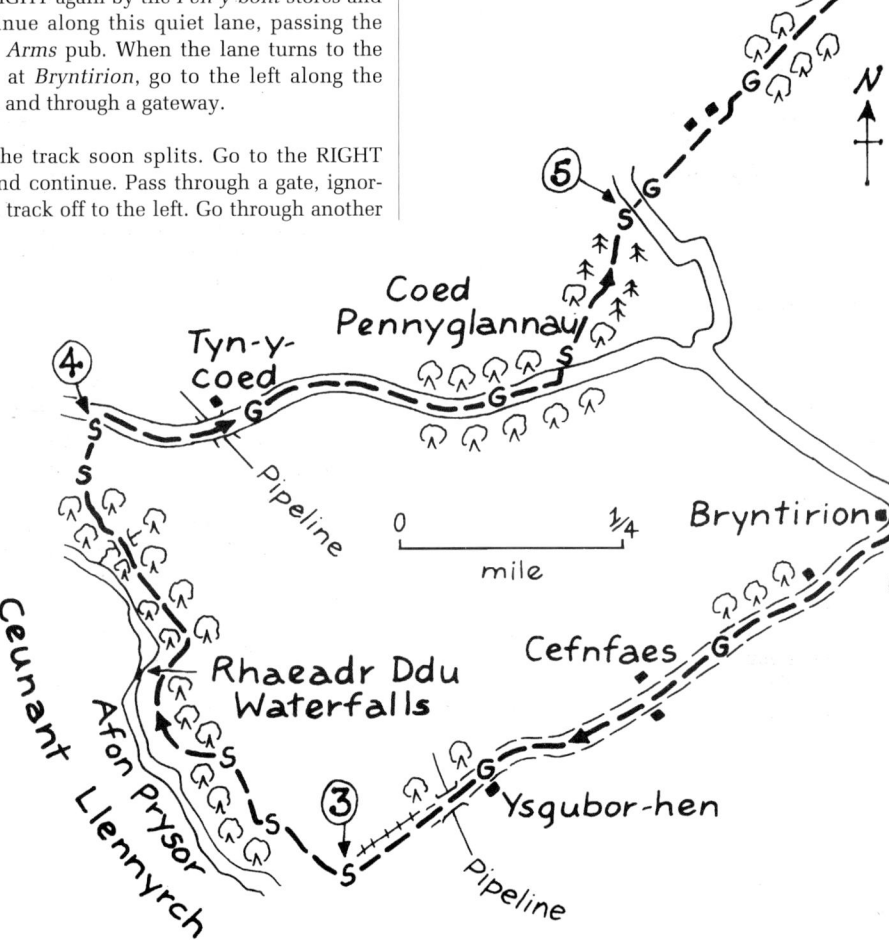

26

WALK 13

gate and soon cross a bridge over an enormous pipe. *This pipe feeds Maentwrog Hydro-Electric Power Station, which has a capacity of 24000 KW, about 1½ miles northwest of here, with water from Llyn Trawsfynydd. This lake is man-made, and dates from 1926. It began supplying 32 million gallons of cooling water each hour to the now defunct nuclear power station at Trawsfynydd in 1965.* Continue straight ahead through a gateway and along the right-hand side of a field.

3 You reach a stile. Cross it and walk half-RIGHT across the field to a stile. Cross this stile into forestry woods, and follow the path around to the right. The path descends towards a stream. Cross the stream and a stile and continue, maintaining your direction downhill when a track crosses. *Just after passing through a gap in a wall, a path branches off to the left. From this you can explore the upper falls BUT TAKE CARE, it is very slippery.* Continue along the track through woods to join another track at a T junction. *Go left for a fine view of the falls.* Turn RIGHT at the junction to continue along a clear path, crossing a footbridge and following the track as it gently climbs the side of the gorge. Eventually the path turns sharp right and rises to a stile. Cross this and continue ahead to a ladder stile.

4 Cross this ladder stile and turn RIGHT to walk along the lane, which again crosses the large pipeline. Go through a gate and continue, passing through a second gate to reach gate and a stile on the LEFT. Cross this stile and follow the path into trees. Eventually you emerge at a stile.

5 Cross this stile, cross the lane and go through the small metal gate opposite. Continue ahead, walking to the right of buildings to reach a ladder stile. Cross this and walk on a path to the left, through trees. Go through a gate by a cottage and continue to join a road. Turn RIGHT to return to Gellilydan.

Rhaeadr-ddu, the Black Waterfall, is one of three such-named waterfalls in Wales. Unfortunately the falls have been greatly depleted by the forming of Llyn Trawsfynydd (see above) and, although sylvan in their setting, the erosion of the surrounding rocks gives a clue to their former glory. This gorge is contained within Ceunant Llenyrch National Nature Reserve, an area noted for fine original oak woods, an example of how the local landscape would have appeared before the trees were cleared for crops. The gorge contains many mosses and liverworts.

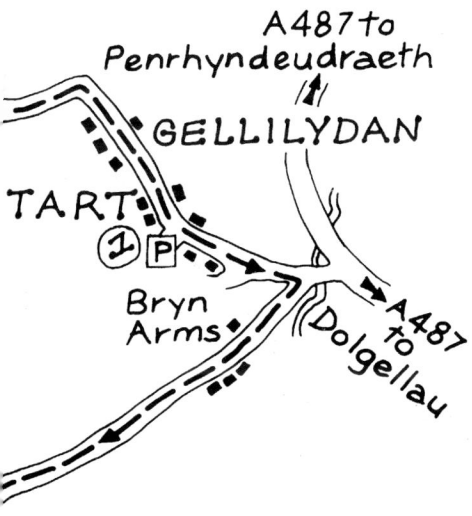

1 Follow the footpath to the LEFT-hand side of the church. Walk by the wall and turn LEFT, to walk down steps. Climb the steps opposite up to a lych-gate, go through and walk up the slope, veering to the RIGHT. Follow the path, which joins a wall on the left. *There is a splendid view over the estuary to the right.* Follow this wall around to

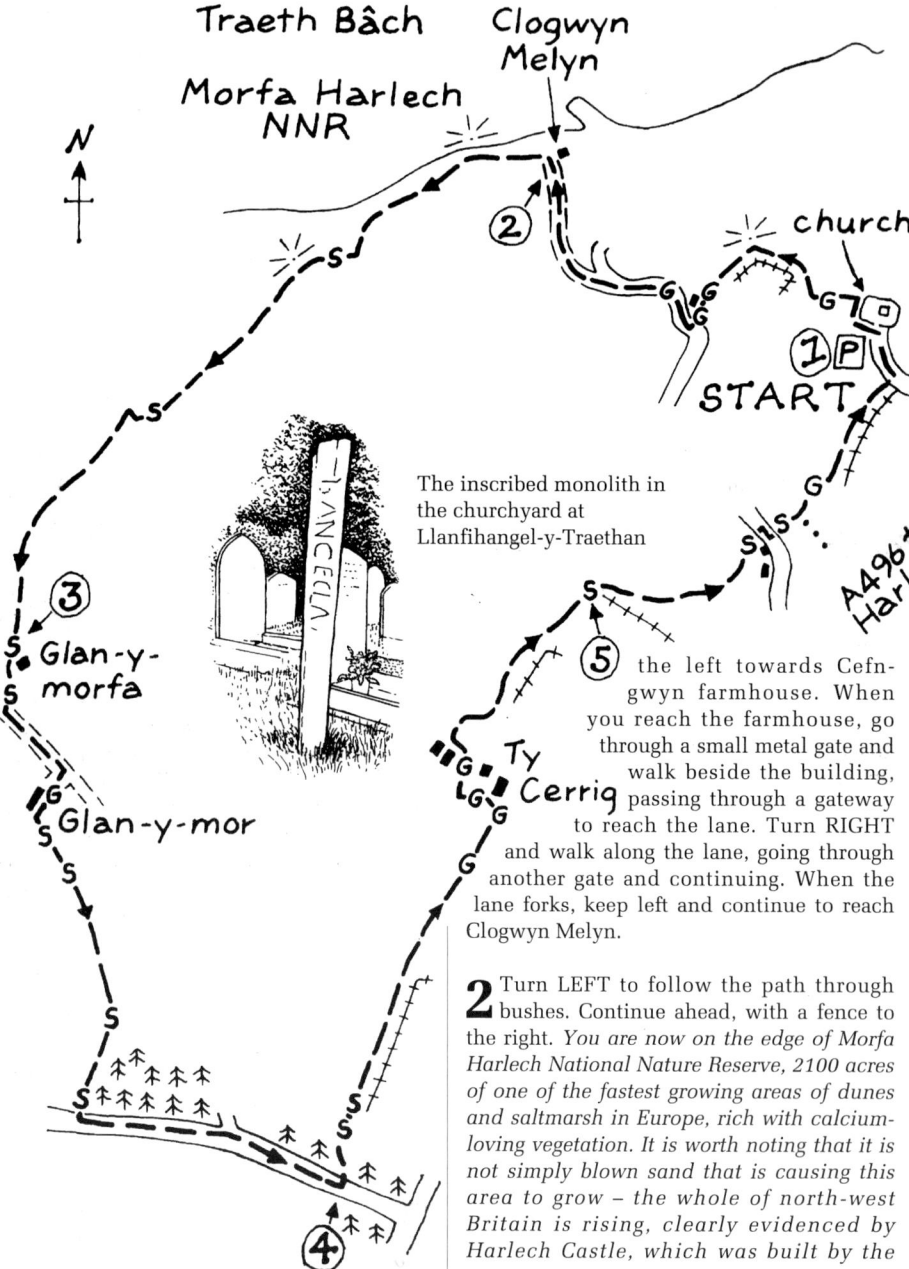

The inscribed monolith in the churchyard at Llanfihangel-y-Traethan

⑤ the left towards Cefngwyn farmhouse. When you reach the farmhouse, go through a small metal gate and walk beside the building, passing through a gateway to reach the lane. Turn RIGHT and walk along the lane, going through another gate and continuing. When the lane forks, keep left and continue to reach Clogwyn Melyn.

2 Turn LEFT to follow the path through bushes. Continue ahead, with a fence to the right. *You are now on the edge of Morfa Harlech National Nature Reserve, 2100 acres of one of the fastest growing areas of dunes and saltmarsh in Europe, rich with calcium-loving vegetation. It is worth noting that it is not simply blown sand that is causing this area to grow – the whole of north-west Britain is rising, clearly evidenced by Harlech Castle, which was built by the*

WALK 14

WALK 14
FROM THE CHURCHYARD AT YNYS

DESCRIPTION A sandy and fairly level 3½-mile route, starting from the ancient church at Ynys. There are superb views across the estuary to Portmeirion (see **Walk 5**), and quiet countryside for the return. Allow about 3 hours.

START The church at Ynys. SH 595354.

DIRECTIONS From the Tourist Information Centre in Porthmadog, take the A487 across The Cob. In Penrhyndeudraeth turn right to cross the toll bridge signed to Harlech. Turn right onto the A496 to reach Ynys. Turn right up the narrow lane signed 'Eglwys Llan-fihangell' and park by the church. Tygwyn British rail station is less than half-a-mile east of Ynys, so you can come by train if you wish.

seashore! During the winter you can see whooper swans, mallard and wigeon; curlew and oystercatcher gather on the mudflats in the north. Go through a gap in a wall and keep the fence to your right, to reach a ladder stile. Cross this and turn LEFT. *You can enjoy a fine view over the estuary from here.* Follow the path ahead, keeping between small hills to reach a ladder stile. Cross the stile and turn RIGHT, then very shortly LEFT as waymarked, walking around the base of hills to the left.

3 Cross a ladder stile and walk in front of *Glan-y-morfa* to a second ladder stile. Cross this and turn LEFT. Go through a gateway (with no gate) and turn RIGHT. Walk through another gateway and cross the farmyard to reach a stile on the LEFT. Cross it and walk half-RIGHT across the field to another stile and cross it. Maintain your direction across the field towards trees. Cross a ladder stile and walk with the trees on your left. Cross another ladder stile and turn LEFT to walk along a concrete road. Continue ahead when a road joins from the left.

4 About 25 yards before reaching trees on the right, turn LEFT onto a path into trees. Cross two ladder stiles and continue ahead, with a fence on your right, maintaining your direction when the fence ends. Go through a gate and continue ahead through another gate and turn LEFT. Go through a gate and veer RIGHT up the track between buildings. Go through a gate and then, after about 25 yards, turn RIGHT along a grassy track. When the fence ends on the right, continue ahead to a stile.

5 Cross the stile and turn RIGHT, to walk with a fence and wall on your right. As you cross the brow of a hill, veer LEFT down towards a signpost to the left of a house. Cross the ladder stile here, cross the lane, and cross the stone step-stile almost opposite. Walk downhill and veer to the LEFT to reach a well-hidden gate on the far side. Go through and continue ahead, picking up a track and walking with a wall to your right. When you reach the lane, turn LEFT to return to the start.

The church of Llanfihangel-y-Traethan, St Michael's on the shores, is considerably older that it would at first appear, having its origins in the 12thC or earlier, when it stood on a tidal island. In 1805 a sea wall was built and much of this low-lying land reclaimed. During the 19thC it was very much a seafarers church in the midst of a boatbuilding area, with yards at Aber-Ia (now Portmeirion), Carreg-y-ro and Ty-Gwyn Gamlas, once the port for Harlech Castle. Unfortunately the church is kept locked, but in the churchyard, to the front of the building, stands a fascinating inscribed monolith about 5 ft tall, dating from the time of King Owain Gwynedd, who reigned 1137-1170. It carries a Latin inscription which reads, when translated: 'Here is the grave of Wledr, mother of Hoedliw who first built this church in the time of King Owain of Gwynedd'. The stone therefore pre-dates Harlech Castle by some 150 years.

WALK 15

WALK 15
LLANDECWYN

DESCRIPTION The church at Llandecwyn commands a superb view over the estuary at Porthmadog, and there is a lovely grassy field beside it for picnics. If you can tear yourself away from this idyllic spot, you could enjoy an easy 2½-mile ramble by a charming lake and through pretty woodlands, before returning up the hill to the church. Allow about 2 hours.

START The church at Llandecwyn. SH 632376.

DIRECTIONS From the Tourist Information Centre in Porthmadog, take the A487 across The Cob. Turn right at Penrhyndeudraeth to cross the Toll Bridge towards Harlech. On the south side of the estuary, drive across the main A496 and continue steeply uphill on a minor road. Turn left at a junction by a telephone box and chapel, and bear left by the lake. Park by the church.

1 From the church, walk back down the hill to Llyn Tecwyn Isaf, and turn sharp LEFT. Continue along the road until it bends left to leave the lake. As it bends left again turn RIGHT to cross a stile into woods. Cross a ladder stile and turn RIGHT, to walk with a wall on your left. Continue ahead along the path, then go through a gate and continue downhill.

2 As you approach *Garth-byr* farm, turn sharp LEFT to go through a gate. Walk down the track to cross a footbridge with a gate and turn LEFT. Step over a small stream and go over a stile. Then walk half-RIGHT on a path up through trees. Go through a gap in a wall and walk diagonally LEFT across the field to a gate. Go through and walk half-LEFT to a gateway into a lane.

3 Go through the gateway and turn LEFT. Walk along the lane and turn RIGHT at the T junction. Continue along the lane.

4 When you reach a short section of stone wall on the left, marking a path uphill, turn sharp LEFT and follow the path. You reach a very handsome step-stile. Cross it and continue along the path ahead. Go through a gate in a fence and carry on, finally descending to the road by the lake. Turn RIGHT to walk back around the lake, then sharp RIGHT to return to the start.

WELSH

The meanings of some of the common words found in local place names

aber	mouth, confluence	foel	bare hill	ogof	cave
afon	river, stream	fynydd	mountain	pandy	fulling mill
allt	hillside	garth	enclosure, hill	pant	hollow
bach	small	glas	green, blue	parc	field, park
banc	hill	glyder	heap	pen	top
blaen	head of valley	glyn	glen	penmaen	rock, promontory
bont	bridge	gors	bog		
bryn	hill	grug	heather	pistyll	waterfall, spout
bwlch	pass	gwen	white		
		gyrn	peak	plas	mansion
cadair (cader)	chair	hafod	summer dwelling	porth	port
caer	fort	hen	old	pwll	pool
capel	chapel	hendre	winter dwelling	rhaeadr	waterfall
castell	castle			rhiw	hill
cefn	ridge	heol	road	rhos	marsh, moor
ceunant	ravine	hir	long		
coch	red			rhyd	ford
coed	wood	isaf	lowest	sarn	road
craig	rock			sych	dry
croes	cross	llan	church		
cwm	valley	llech	slate	tarren	hill
		llidiart	gate	tomen	mound
dinas	fort, city	llwyd	grey	traeth	shore, beach
dol	meadow	llyn	lake		
du	black			traws	across
dwr	water	maen	stone	tref	hamlet, home
dyffryn	valley	maes	field		
		mawr	big	twll	hole
eglwys	church	melin	mill	ty	house
esgair	hillspur	moch	pigs		
		moel	bare hill	uchaf	highest
fach	small	mor	sea		
fan	high place	mynach	monk	y, yr	the, of the
fawr	large	mynydd	mountain	ynys	island
fechan	small			ysgol	school
felin	mill	nant	stream	ystrad	valley floor
ffordd	road	neuadd	hall		
ffynnon	spring, well	newydd	new		

PRONUNCIATION

These basic points should help non-Welsh speakers

Welsh	English equivalent
c	always hard, as in **c**at
ch	as on the Scottish word lo**ch**
dd	as th in **th**en
f	as v in **v**ocal
ff	as **f**
g	always hard as in **g**ot
ll	no real equivalent. It is like 'th' in **th**en, but with an 'L' sound added to it, giving '**thlan**' for the pronunciation of the Welsh 'Llan'.

In Welsh the accent usually falls on the last-but-one syllable of a word.

KEY TO THE MAPS

- ➔ Walk route and direction
- ═ Metalled road
- ⁻⁻⁻ Unsurfaced road
- ╪╪╪ Fenced track (fence/hedge)
- ∞∞∞ Wall
- •••• Footpath/route adjoining walk route
- ■▭■ Railway
- ⌇⌇➔ River/stream & flow
- ♣ ♤ Trees
- ↻ Shrub/bracken/gorse
- **G** Gate
- **S** Stile
- F.B. Footbridge
- ⸽⸽ Viewpoint
- **P** Parking
- **T** Telephone
- **i** Tourist Information Centre

Published by
Kittiwake 3 Glantwymyn Village Workshops, nr Machynlleth, Montgomeryshire SY20 8LY

© *Text*: David Perrott 1999
© *Maps*: Kittiwake Press 1999

THE COUNTRY CODE

Enjoy the countryside and respect its life and work

Guard against all risk of fire

Leave gates *as you find them*

Keep your dogs under close control

Keep to public paths across farmland

Use gates and stiles to cross fences, hedges and walls

Leave livestock, crops and machinery alone

Take your litter home

Help to keep all water clean

Protect wildlife, plants and trees

Take special care on country roads

Make no unnecessary noise

Maps and illustrations: Morag Perrott

We would like to thank The Snowdonia National Park Authority, who have checked all of the walks which fall within The Park area, and the Ffestiniog Railway, who also provided assistance.
Created on an Macintosh, using Works, Freehand, Photoshop and QuarkXPress
Printed by Artists Valley Press, Machynlleth

ISBN: **1 902302 00 1**